Poems and Verse of Winifred Holtby

Edited by

Antony Webb

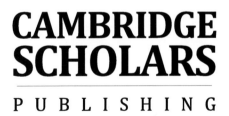

CAMBRIDGE SCHOLARS

PUBLISHING

Poems and Verse of Winifred Holtby,
Edited by Antony Webb

This book first published 2012

Cambridge Scholars Publishing

12 Back Chapman Street, Newcastle upon Tyne, NE6 2XX, UK

British Library Cataloguing in Publication Data
A catalogue record for this book is available from the British Library

ISBN (10): 1-4438-4000-9, ISBN (13): 978-1-4438-4000-2

121313

Poems and Verse of Winifred Holtby

This book is dedicated to my wife Jacqueline who was responsible for the correction of the text of the poems which were taken direct from Winifred Holtby's private papers.

CONTENTS

Table of Contents

ACKNOWLEDGEMENTS

I would like to thank Marion Shaw, Literary Executor for Winifred Holtby for giving her permission to allow publication of this book.

I owe many thanks to Patricia West, who was responsible for starting me on this journey of discovery, after her attending a literary evening in Norwich where the guest speaker was Baroness Shirley Williams (the daughter of Vera Brittain and close friend of Winifred Holtby).

I would also like to thank Martin Taylor and his staff at the Hull University History Centre, especially Nicola Herbert, Kath Stephenson, Carol Williams, Michel Beadle, Joanne Chilman and Angela-Hurd Shaw for their help in my research of the Winifred Holtby Archive.

Also I am indebted to the help given to me by the staff of the Norwich Millennium library and Great Yarmouth library.

Also Keran Webb who has been actively engaged in checking the manuscript and advising on IT matters.

FOREWORD

DAME SHIRLEY WILLIAMS

Winifred Holtby, a woman whose radiant and generous personality inspired friendship in many of the people who met her, was not known primarily as a poet. We are all in Mr. Webb's debt for painstakingly compiling this collection of her poems. Her novels bore witness to her gift for prose, lightened by humour, empathy for her fellow human beings and a remarkable capacity for description. By the time of her early death at the age of thirty seven, she was just reaching her full potential. Her final book, *South Riding*, showed just how rich that potential was.

Her poetry reflected the pattern of her life, the experiences that dominated each particular stage. Her childhood, spent in the rolling wolds of the East Riding of Yorkshire, fertile countryside once ravaged and pillaged by the Vikings, was shaped by the seasons and the vagaries of nature. Her father, a substantial farmer, taught her about agriculture as she accompanied him on his tours of his land. For much of her childhood, farming suffered a serious depression, reflected long after in her descriptions of the poverty of smallholders in *South Riding*.

Her early poems, several of them written as a schoolgirl, are touching but not remarkable. The exception is *Question and Answer*, written when she was about thirteen. She asks in it why she should suffer and struggle. The date of writing must have been around the time she caught scarlet fever at her boarding school, a serious illness that left a long legacy of ill health including renal failure.

The poem that captures the immemorial quality of traditional agriculture, the sowing, the reaping and the harvest, is *Harvest at Anlaby*. The poem reads like a lullaby, the repetition reminiscent of familiar music. The same theme of a golden harvest is repeated in a poem written four years later, when the First World War was already a year old, *The Harvest Fields of Fair Lorraine*. But now the horrors of war mutilate the harvest: "And midst the gold are crimson stains, the blood of slaughtered men".

The War was not as devastating for Winifred as it was for her beloved friend Vera Brittain. Yet she shared the grief of my mother's bereavements, as her poem *The Frozen Earth* shows. The greatest of them was the death of Edward, Vera's only brother, in Italy shortly before the war ended:

> "And you are not there, not there, not there,
> Your laughing face and your windblown hair
> Leave not even a ghost in the garden"

Winifred's love and empathy were surprisingly matched by a sharp and perceptive wit. Two of the poems of her twenties exemplify this rare combination, the ingenuous *Warning*, a poem about my father's learned and scholarly local priest, Father de Zulueta, and the sensitive and moving *The Foolish Clocks*. Her poetic gifts grow and mature with her journey to South Africa in 1926, a country she found both enchanting and painful, the beauty of its scenery challenged by the bigotry and sourness of its system of apartheid. Memories of earlier experiences also demanded a deeper poetic expression in these years. One of the finest is the haunting *Trains in France*; another, *The Symphony Concert*, harks back to the loss of Edward, who yearned to be a violinist. Then there are the poems such as *The Robber* and *Beauty: The Way of the World*, recalling her youthful love for a young Yorkshireman, Harry Pearson, a love that crackled and sputtered like coals in a dying fire for the rest of her life.

Some of these poems are clearly influenced by other contemporary poets. *The Dead Man*, written in Oxford when Winifred was a student at the University there, could have been written by A.E Housman. Many years later, *House on Fire*, written in 1932, comparing the short life of a house on fire with joy with one built on grief and sorrow, reminded me of Edna St Vincent Millay, my father's favourite poet, which he may well have discussed with Winifred:

> "On the solid rocks the houses of my neighbours stand
> Come and see my shining palace built upon the sand"

The last poems in this collection, *The Ghost of Elinor Wylie* and *Valley of Shadows* provide us with intimations of what we have lost. Elinor Wylie, an American poet, suffered from a similar illness to Winifred's. The three poems dedicated to her bear witness to the suffering Winifred also endured as a result of Bright's disease, the successor to scarlet fever. In *Valley of Shadows*, the young poet is beginning to come to terms with the prospect of her early death and the wild hope of being reunited in the after-life with

Vera, and perhaps with Harry Pearson too.

Those who knew Winifred, whether in life or through her books, will treasure this collection, both for the light it throws on her own self, and also for the intimations of the poet she might have become.

INTRODUCTION

Winifred Holtby was born at Rudston, East Yorkshire on the 23rd June 1898 she died on the 29th September 1935. During her short life she wrote several books, Anderby Wold, Land of Green Ginger, Poor Caroline, Mandoa Mandoa and her most famous South Riding. She was also a prolific writer of letters, poems and verse. She put many of her poems into the letters she wrote to her friends. But at her death the only published work of poetry was a small volume of poems called My Garden and Other Poems, that her mother Alice Holtby took from the scraps of paper that she threw into her waste paper basket unknown to Winifred.

After her first book of poems, even though Winifred wrote many others, but no other book was published in her life time. In the year of her death Collins published the Frozen Earth and other Poems but only containing 16 of her poems. Collins in the forward to the book admitted that there were many other poems and verse written by Winifred Holtby, but they were scattered amongst her letters and within back issues of newspapers and magazines and it required someone to undertake research in order to bring them together under one volume. It is hoped that this book will act as a definitive work of her poetry.

Winifred Holtby's poems act as markers through out her life, initially whilst still at school apart from My Garden and Other Poems, she also wrote, QMS Scarborough and the Harvest Fields of Fair Lorraine. When she went up to Oxford University she wrote the Harvest at Anlaby which pointed towards her first novel Anderby Wold. This was a story about the East Riding of Yorkshire, where Winifred grew up. Some very poignant poems were written when she was going through difficult periods in her relationship with Harry Pearson the "Boy friend that isn't a boy friend", caused by his inability to make a commitment to Winifred. Through out her life he would suddenly appear, normally out of work and she would support him financially and materially. Then he would just disappear not telling her where he was, through out her life he took everything and gave her nothing in return. From this relationship she wrote, The Robber, The Dead Man, Epilogue to Romance, Grudging Ghost and Epigram to the End of Love, all of which show the pain that she went through with this man.

The poem Trains in France relates to a time when she was in the WAAC in France in 1918. As a hostel Forewoman she was taking the women who worked for her to their posting in Camiers, spending an uncomfortable night in a goods van, she never forgot the sound of the trains as screamed by.

The very lovely verse of Epigram to Vera Brittain, indicated the close friendship that these two women had. The poem Hills of the Transvaal represents her time in South Africa, where she spent six months by herself lecturing on behalf of the League of Nations Union to trades union, in their struggle against the colour bar, in order to obtain equality with white workers. She continued this work after her return to England and raised considerable funds to support this cause, sending out William Ballinger as her representative.

Towards the end of her life, when she was suffering from the chronic symptoms of Brights Disease (Renal Failure). She wrote three moving poems for the Ghost of Elinor Wylie. Elinor Wylie an American Poetess who suffered from a disease similar to that of Winifred's. Within these poems she tells of the symptoms and pain that racked her body. Yet she managed to continue in the work that she loved in writing novels and journalism, completing also the manuscript for South Riding just two weeks before her death.

One of the last poems in this book The Valley of the Shadows recently discovered in Winifred Holtby's Archive at Hull University. This very moving poem was obviously written shortly before her death. In it Winifred is giving thanks to a special person who has helped and supported her throughout her adult life. This person saw her through difficult times, especially when her health was at a low ebb. This was the person who held the bowl whilst she was being violently ill. Although Winifred became an agnostic whilst at Oxford University, in this poem she shows respect for this special person's beliefs. "For in a little while we meet again". This special person can only be her close friend Vera Brittain.

JEALOUS GHOST

My feet are treading the long green meadows
My body swims on the cool green sea.
The sliding shadows of twilight cover
The sunsets crimson, delighting me.

These winds and waters, the summer pleasures
Were yours for the taking if you choose
No hoarded treasures that I must ransom,
By more forsaking what you would lose.

Ah ghost, grey ghost in the dark earth lying
Was there no rapture to keep you there?
Must you in dying steal joy for ever.
And jealous, capture the sweet o' the year

Winifred Holtby, Hull

BERKSHIRE RAIN

The coloured clouds on polar stems
 Uncurl above the dripping trees:
While moving slowly down the Thames
Go swans more flower-like than these,
 As though lilies taller grew
And blossomed into cloudy flowers
Then, wind blown, poured their load of dew
Upon the street, in birds and showers.

Thus Leda came, and on the green
Dark water saw her floating swan,
And thought she has a lily seen,
So waved her hand, and wandered on,
Demeter's daughter passing by,
Saw clouds like lilies budding there
So plucked the blossom from the sky
And wore it in her rain-wet hair.

Winifred Holtby
Hull

TREASURE IN HEAVEN

I had an hour, a darling eager hour;
Time, you cannot touch it; this is mine, mine, mine,
An hour of dahlias and poetry and elephants

I had an hour, a secret, silver hour;
All the trees were singing songs I could not understand,
Cedars sycamores, laburnums and acacias,
While the sun rose shyly on the unknown land.

I had an hour, my love was here one hour,
She it was who smiled at me, hers the voice I heard,
Hers the gown of green and gold, hers the laughter
Hers the head as soft to kiss as feathers of a bird
Magical.

These are my treasure, these are my dominions;
Moth and rust cannot corrupt nor thief break through
and steal
Rich beyond all reckoning, glorious, secure am I,
Rich am I in heaven, these immortal joys I feel.

Winifred Holtby
Hull

THE DEBT

I Owe so large a debt to life;
I think if I should die to-day
My death would never quite repay
For music, friends and careless laughter,
The swift, light-hearted interplay
Of wit on ready wit, and after,
The silence that most blessed falls
Across the room and fire lit walls
And quells our flame of jesting strife.
I owe so large a debt to life
No gift can wipe it away
Nor any tears that I can borrow
From watching all the world's wild sorrow,
As autumn never can allay
The promise of a sunlit morrow
We had a legacy from May.
 I owe so large a debt to life
That I am bankrupt evermore
While Misery about my door
Stops, hungry eyed, to stand and pray
That I should give him of my store.
"Oh, Misery" I cry, "Away!
Why come you begging from a debtor?
Whate'er I give is not my own,
To seek at other doors were better.
You should have begged from such as they
Won nightly weep with bitter tears
The glory of their wasted years.
They hold credit still with fate,
Go forth and ask them for a loan."
But Misery, importunate,
Before me sweeps and will not wait,
Standing in sorrow at my gate,
While in the wind his tatters sway
And from his wrist clanks fear's harsh fetter.

And I must listen to his moan;
He holds before my heart a knife,
And threatens me to buy or borrow.
But only sorrow gives to sorrow.
How can I give, who am a debtor?
I owe too large a debt to life,

Winifred Holtby 1923

The next six poems are of Winifred Holtby's early work.

ON SAD ASCENSION DAY

Mourning Mother weep no more
O'er my uncles death so sore,
Others need your care much more
Than he.

He is in heaven is at rest
Leaning on Lord Jesu's breast
He is now forever blest
Up There.

Far' way ore the crystal sea
There a place is kept for thee,
Father, Kitty, Grace and me
With him.

Winifred Holtby aged 8 (1910)

ONLY

Only a rose-bud
Tender and soft
Dropped from a tree
Waving aloft.

Only a kind thought
Spoken by love,
Dropped like a rosebud
From heaven above.

But the wee rose bud
Once pleasure gave,
The kind thought's remembered
Unto the grave

Written by Winifred Holtby 1910
Hull

QUESTION AND ANSWER

Oh, how long is the path and how weary the struggle!
The road is so rough and so steep.
Oh! How far must I must, climb and how long must I
suffer
Before I can lay me to sleep?

Oh, why should I suffer? Oh, why should I struggle,
When fame is a calling to me?
Oh, why should I toil in the murk of the city
When I hear the grand roar of the sea?

Winifred Holtby 1911

WHY SHOULD WE MORTALS

Why should we mortals rulers of this world
Bow down ourselves to One who went before
And is long dead - One who has passed before,
Whom we have never seen, nor can see
Till the last trumpet should sound, proclaiming all
At end, Both land and sea, and beasts and men
All mortals to be ended, and the world,
And all the universe, one bare blank space,
Devoid of light, of life, of everything
Save his own presence, making all things day;
And life and love perpetually there.
The end of all things, save of Him Himself.

Winifred Holtby Aged 11

Q.M.S Scarborough

There's a long grey school on a windswept hillside,
Where over garden the wild sea-birds cry:
There's a red roofed town that waves wash ever
And a castle stands guarding it really high.
And far away from the eastward coast line,
Where the wind from the moor land heights blows chill,
We suddenly pause in our work to remember
That red roofed town at the foot of the hill.

When the valley lies still in the soft morning sunlight,
And the looped river gleams like a silver snake,
And the misty clouds that unwraps the shoulders
Of the mountain giants grow tattered and break,
Then we think of the waves in the golden morning,
When the great sun rises beyond the sea,
Throwing living flame on the grey, cold waters,
And the fresh salt sting of the wind blowing free.

Winifred Holtby (Aged 151/2)
Queen Margaret's School Magazine 1915

THE HARVEST FIELDS OF FAIR LORRAINE

The Harvest fields of fair Lorraine
Were Crowded with yellow corn,
And amidst the gold were crimson heads
By poppy stems up borne.
In dewy morn the peasants reap,
In quivering heat of noon,
Till o'er the purple hill-top glides
The primrose harvest moon.
The harvest fields of fair Lorraine
Are not so gold as then,
And midst the gold as then,
And midst the gold are crimson stains,
The blood of slaughtered men;
And by the light of one lone star
And the chill wind's sobbing breath
A reaper gathers his harvest there-
And the reapers name is death.

From the Play Espinage by Winifred Holtby 1915

MY PRAYER

Lord grant me grace
That I may ever keep a little space
Within my heart, for all defilement free,
And consecrate it, Lord of light, to these
That I may go.

And rest awhile within, and ever know
That for our petty woes and pains apart
Thou ever waitest for me, in my heart,
that I may take.

A flame from beauty's altar and may make
A lighted shrine for ever burning fair
So I may steal away and worship there
Oh Lord I plead.

That I may turn aside, in better need
Stifled by spite and ugliness and strife
And all the small, distasteful tasks of life
And may there find.

A shrine to beauty hidden in my mind:
Where sweet refreshment on my heart shall fall
The gracious love that understandable all
Thus may I turn.

Face foremost where the fires most fiercely burn
And greet each coming hour with a smile
Feeling thy strong companionship the while.

Winifred Holtby 1918

No Mourning by Request

Come not to mourn for me with solemn tread
Clad in dull weeds of sad sable hue,
Nor weep because my tale of life's told through,
Casting light dust on my untroubled head.
Nor linger near me while the sexton fills
My grave with earth—but go gay-garlanded,
And in your halls a shining banquet spread
And gild your chamber o'er with daffodils.

Fill your tall goblets with white wine and red,
And sing brave songs of gallant love and true,
Wearing soft robes of emerald and blue,
And dance, as I your dances oft have led,
And laugh, as I have often laughed with you—
And be most merry—after I am dead.

Winifred Holtby 1923

THE HARVEST AT ANLABY

The heavy wains slow moving go
Across the broad autumnal wold
To great brown-throated men below
Who gather in the glowing gold.

And thus it was they harvested,
They harvested at Anlaby
Before the Danes from Bessingly
Flooded the manor like the sea,
And left Earl Godwin's barley red—
At Anlaby.

The lovers linger down the lane
When moths awake and small owls cry.
Their dresses fade, as pale moons wane,
And glimmer as they wander by.

And thus it was they made their vows at Anlaby,
When all the wolds were young as they
Amongst the dusky sheaves they lay,
And kissed beneath the darkened boughs
At Anlaby

Winifred Holtby 1920

THE QUEST

I searched for happiness at break of day,
While one pale star still lit the morning's grey.
My heart was filled with passion of desire,
The rapture of my ardours burned like fire
I left my home, and friends and wealth behind
And journeyed out, life's happiness to find.

I looked for happiness in fames great court,
But wealth and honour brought not what I sought
I heard the populace applaud my name,
At cost of liberty I bought my fame.
But chains of gold bound tight to earth my soul,
And power was bitter. This was not my goal.

I next drank deep draughts of sparkling wine,
I saw a Rose and longed for to make it mine,
But surely I this precious flower might wear.
It swung too high. I counted not the cost,
So made a silken rope of honours lost.
Up this I climbed, and plucked the Rose so fair,
But underneath its bloom, sharp thorns lay there.

Wearied of glory bought at freedoms cost,
Tired of love fulfilled with honours lost,
I found a cloister, peaceful and cool and grey,
And thus I paid my penance day by day.
Too late I raised to heaven my tearful cry.
The cloisters peace was not for such as I.

Now weary of the toil and of the quest,
I seek me but a little place to rest.
A narrow house in which to lay my head
Amid the silent gardens of the dead,
A long calm sleep until Judgement Day
Where lies happiness no man can say.

Winifred Holtby Hull

FLOODLIGHTS ON THE CANCER HOSPITAL

Here is the Place
Out from engulfing darkness, sharply white
Glares the metallic light,
Illuminating wall and gilded sign,
A dreadful word branded across its face
Here is the Place.

How brave is Man
Who challenges the impenetrable night
With his obedient light,
Who builds of glass and steel his towering walls
Bending earth, fire and air to serve his plan
How brave is man.

From the great dark
From the deep forest, from the primeval slime
Undaunted does he climb,
Harmonising his to his needs the invisible air,
From molten earth to build his sheltering ark,
From the great dark.

And this is all
The instrument his undefeated spirit owns
A feeble case of flesh and blood and bones,
Enslaved to time, suffering earth's decay;
Burn it, it shrivels; strike it, it will fall--
And this is all.

Yet unafraid
Here he has reared his palaces of power
Built to endure all hours,
As though all life were under his control,
These things at least his feeble hands have made,
Yet unafraid.

He has disowned
The stoics mute endurance, he will try
To twist the stars from the reluctant sky,
To alter destiny, to mould his proper fate,
The humbler need docile acceptance loaned
He has disowned

Yet here we pause,
Before this vast repository of pain,
The baffled spirit checks and turns again
Then flings its electric challenge to the night
Our skill we carry through the opening doors,
Yet here we pause

This is the end
For all our skill we have not conquered death
Our spirit leaves our bodies within our final breath.
We lay our instrument of flesh aside
When hurt beyond all mortal hope to end
This is the end

Winifred Holtby
Hull

IGNIS FATUUS

I hear you singing through the summer rain
Mournful and low, a half-forgotten air,
Of women wailing through their fallen hair,
Or dead leaves drifting down a dreary plain.
And long ago when Babylon was fair
Listening I lay within a marble hall
Watching the rainbow-dripping fountain fall,
And rose to follow your soft singing there.
Lonely from star to star I follow still,
Lured by an echo, while about me lie
The ghosts of spinning worlds that leap and die.
Untouched by time, from starlit hill to hill
You lead me, till alone we traverse soon,
Remote and dead, the mountains of the moon.

Winifred Holtby 1920

THE SARABANDE

A Coward's Apology

So you are angry, will not take my hand,
Nor laugh to me again with loving eyes;
But lift your charming head with hurts surprise,
Half scornful. Dear, you do not understand.
Down music-haunted halls we bow and sway,
Moving in measured figures, gravely planned;
Not knowing what wild air the minstrels play.
You hid your anger with disdainful face
Thinking twas I who gave the sidelong glance,
Tortured your soul upon a turn of chance.
Because I trod my measure out of place
You thought I wittingly forwent your grace.
It was not I, dear heart. It was the dance.

Winifred Holtby 1920

THE DEAD MAN

I see men walk wild ways with love,
Along the wind their laughter blown
Strikes up against the singing stars—
But I lie alone.

When love has stricken laughter dead
And tears their silly hearts in twain,
They long for easeful death, but I
Am hungry for their pain.

Taken from Oxford Poetry
Winifred Holtby 1920

THE SHIP BUILDER

If all my ships put out to sea
And never came to me,
And I should watch from day to day
The empty waste of waters grey--
Then I would fashion one ship more
Of broken driftwood from the shore,
And build it up with toil and pain
And send it out to sea again.
With this last ship upon the sea
I'd turn and laugh right merrily.

Winifred Holtby 1920

O DREAMY, GLOOMY, FRIENDLY TREES

O dreamy, gloomy, friendly trees
I came along your narrow track
To bring my gifts unto your knees,
And gifts did you give back.
For when I brought this heart that burns --
These thoughts that bitterly repine--
And laid them here among the ferns
And the hum of the boughs divine,
Ye vastest breathers of the air,
Shook down with slow and mighty poise
Your coolness on the human care
Your wonder on its joys--
Your greenness on the hearts despair,
Your darkness on its noise.

Winifred Holtby 1920

VAGABOND LOVE

Love is a vagabond
Roving at will
All round the world, over
Valley and hill.

Should he pass by your door
 Pretty maids, pray
Call to him cunningly,
Bid him to stay.

Snare him with loveliness,
Coax him with Joy,
Blue beads, and gold for a
Fugitive boy.

Did you not hear but now
Light footsteps fall --
Laughter along the road
Clear as birds call?

Little he's guessing that
I'll have him soon--
I built a house for him
Under the moon.

There, with dark moss below,
Small stars above,
I'll hold him prisoner,
Vagabond love.

Winifred Holtby 1920

THE DIM BROWN WOODS ARE WEEPING

The dim brown woods are weeping
Beneath an ashen sky:
On branches swinging
The last pale leaves are clinging,
Before, with thrifty reaping
The cold winds bears them by,
When dim brown woods are weeping
Beneath an ashen sky.

Their golden treasure squandered
The trees are stark and bare.
No promise born of May time
Rings through the dreary day time:
No beggared by despair,
Their golden treasure squandered,
The trees are stark.

Of beauty followed blindly,
Of beauty that must die
Can we not store the treasure,
Has losing them no measure,
Or must we love so kindly
And loving, pass it by?
Of beauty followed blindly,
Of beauty that must die.

When my heart remembers
The glory that was May
Has life no gift of laughter
For what may follow after?
What care we for Decembers
That March winds waft away,
When my heart remembers
The glory that was May?

This poem written by Winifred Holtby 1920 was based on Swinburnes
The Sea Mew.

EPILOGUE TO ROMANCE

I would not honour love the less,
Who know myself to be
Unworthy of the tenderness
Of your sweet constancy;
But walk more proudly on my way alone,
Because you once loved me.

I shall go gaily all my days
Where skies are wild and blue,
Finding the flowers about my ways
Are clad in richer hue—
And in the darkest night one star will burn
Because I once loved you.

Why should I weep for one short day
That you have passed my door?
No changing time can snatch away
The joy that went before.
I shall be thankful all my life for love
Although we love no more.

Winifred Holtby 1921

THE ROBBER

If dreams were true, then you would come today
And find Love's habitation desolate;
I think his wayward fancy would not wait
For your return, when you were far away.
But I sit lonely with my heart all bare;
When others come and knock upon the door
Only there shadows cross the empty floor,
And fade again, because you are not there.
For when you went away, Love said good bye,
Fled from my heart, and left the door ajar,
Seeking your fleeting form from star to star
Until he find you, or not finding, die.
And I have neither happiness nor pain
Until you come and bring me love again.

Winifred Holtby 1921

THE LAZY POET

Why should I a poet be?
All the flowers sing for me;
Every bird and every tree
Sings a dancing melody.
Songs he knew when Eve was young
Tumble from the blue-tit's tongue.
 Mournful choirs of midges croon
All the golden afternoon.
Furry bees and nimble crickets
Hide around the briar thickets,
While the round and idle sun,
With his working day half done,
 Lays his head upon a cloud,
 Laughing slyly, laughing loud.
 I can hear the chestnut trees,
 Hardly stirring in the breeze,
 Murmur sleepy lullabies
To the lazy, languid flies.
 I can hear the river go
 In the valley far below
Singing softly in the grass
And floating leaves that pass
 Little songs that rise and fall.
 I can hear a silver call
 From hanging flower-bells
 Flinging sweet and plaintive spells
For the clumsy, questing bees,
Ringing slowly ding, dong, ding!
All the songs that I could sing
Are not half so fine as these.
Why should I a poet be?
All the flowers sing for me.

Winifred Holtby 1922

EPIGRAM TO VERA BRITTAIN

Sweet Pilgrim, since awhile I walked with thee,
My fortune's thine, while thine brings wealth to me.
Now so enriched am I that I remain
Not poorer, sweet, but richer for thy gain.

Winifred Holtby 1924

FROZEN EARTH

"Edwards Funeral March"

As I come through the garden,
Suddenly all birds seem to cease their singing:
The tight-curled buds like birds on the branches swinging
Silently shrink and harden
On the naked trees that were once green fountains springing.
And you are not there, not there, not there,
Your laughing face and your windblown hair
Leave not even a ghost in the garden.

So how can I remember
What you were like in the spring when birds were crying
And the call of your voice, and the sound of
Your footsteps flying?
The garden in December
Is frozen too hard for the lads in the dark earth lying
To wander again, again, again,
As blithe as bird-song and light as rain
That I may see and remember.

Winifred Holtby 1925

Note: Edward is referring to Vera Brittains brother who was killed on the
Asiago Plateau, Italy, 1918.

INVOCATION TO TIME

O Time, deal gently with me.
I cannot see the colours of the wind
Where green lands of blossom from unshadowed seas.
Their music beckons, but I cannot find
The dark cathedral of the forest trees,
Nor from the night's deep chalice for my healing
Drink wine of strange communion, blindly kneeling
To pray from your omnipotence one hour
That will not perish, one immortal flower.
O Time, deal gently with me.

Winifred Holtby 1925

ARABIA

Sweet is the music of Arabia
In my heart, when out of dreams
I still in the thin clear murk of dawn
Descry her gliding streams;
Hear her strange lutes on the green banks
Ring loud with grief and delight
Of the dim-silken, dark-haired musicians
In the brooding silence of night.

They haunt me--her lutes and her forests,
No beauty on earth I see
But shadowed with that dream recalls
Her loveliness to me:
Still eyes look coldly upon me,
Cold voices whisper and say—
He is crazed with the spell of far Arabia,
They have stolen his wits away.

Winifred Holtby 1925

THE BENEFACTRESS

My neighbour on her window -sill
Has set a nodding daffodil,
I laugh to see it blowing there
Golden and tall and debonair.
The boys and girls who never saw
So green and gold a thing before
Here linger with enchanted feet
To watch Spring Flowering down our street.
But Arthur says he knew a hill
Between the Somme and Huchennville
When golden daffodils were gay-
Once, far away -long years away.
And Yorkshire Dick can close his eyes
And see the wooded uplands rise,
With daffodils more gold than these
Gleaming like sunlight through the trees.

For Emma on her window-sill
Has set a nodding daffodil.

Winifred Holtby 1925

THE TRAVELLERS

See, I have cast my nets
Over the ball of the world.
Wherever my friends sail out on the wide seas,
Wherever their sails are furled
In hill-girt harbour, or swinging river-mouth,
My nets are hurled.

The ships bring news for me,
And the wind their words,
For my friends have enslaved the trees as their messengers,
The slow moving herds
Of cattle, the wind-blown seeds, and the running streams,
And the homing birds.

Now all the world is mine,
China and Labrador,
Hungary, Africa, Washington, Rome,
And a hundred more
Tall cities, and many a sudden-flowering isle
And rocky shore.

For I have part in the land
Wherever my friends go.
Wherever the hills of their pilgrimage break and their cities tower
And their red roads glow,
I have cast my nets and drawn them home to my mind,
Though they never know.

Now I am rich indeed
Who hold half earth in fee.
There is not a flowering field in all the world
Not an almond tree,
But its beauty has gladdened the heart of a friend of mine,
And enriches.

Winifred Holtby 1926

HILLS OF THE TRANSVAAL

Stark in the morning sun's unwinking stare
The naked hills lie agonised with shame
Feeling their umber loins and shoulders bare
Beneath the scorching insult of its flame
Like exiled Adam, helplessly aware
Of Vanished Paradise, below the deep
Unmoving meadows of the ocean, where
In hidden innocence they lay asleep.

But when the quiet evening comes, they seem
Like exiles comforted, to take their ease,
Naked no longer then they lie and dream
Girdled with shadow and twilit trees,
Watching as in a mirror fade and gleam
Their unforgotten Eden of the seas.

Winifred Holtby 1926

MANOA

Whilst my soul like quiet palmer
Travelleth towards the land of Heaven

Over the silver mountains
Where spring the nectar fountains,
There will I kiss the bowl of bliss
And drink mine everlasting fill
Upon every milken hill.

My soul will be a dry before,
But after, it will thirst no more

Taken from Sir Walter Raleigh's Manoa by Winifred Holtby, 1927.

A LADY IN A LITTLE GARDEN IN KENSINGTON

A Lady in a Little Garden in Kensington
So calm indeed, she seemed, and good
It was as if an angel stood
Dreaming through paradisal hours
With folded wings among the flowers.

Winifred Holtby 1925

THERE'S A HALL IN BLOOMSBURY

And there's a hall in Bloomsbury
No more I dare to tread,
For all the stone men shout at me
and swear they are not dead.
And once I touched a marble girl,
and knew that marble bled."

Winifred Holtby 1925

GENTILITY

When vines go prancing hand in hand
Down sunny slopes of Southern land,
When reeling hops with tangled tresses
Splash crimson stains across their dresses,
And flaunting yellow dahlias try
To woo the Sun's enamoured eye,
Where lately lolled the drunken sheaves
In stooks as broad as browsing beeves,
I hear a hymn of harvest born
From Sabbath, fields all newly shorn.
Now sleek and smooth, they clearly feel
That Emptiness is more genteel.

Winifred Holtby 1925

DRAMA

All day
I see the house - walls blind and grey

Inside
 Nothing is there for them to hide
 But dusty fern and a ribbon tied
 In a petticoat-knot round the curtain.

At night
Windows suddenly leap to light;

I see
White laid tables and shrimps for tea
and men and women who don't see me,
But who twisted the knot round the curtain.

Winifred Holtby 1925

THE FOOLISH CLOCKS

Now she is gone, but all her clocks are ticking
With gentle voices, punctual and polite,
Their thrifty hands the scattered moments picking,
Tossed from the careless bounty of the night.

Oh, foolish clocks, who had no wit for hoarding
The precious moments when my love was here,
Be silent now, and cease this vain recording
Of worthless hours, since she is not near.

Winifred Holtby 1925

PRAYER

Oh time deal gently with me.
I cannot see the colours of the wind
Where green lands blossom from un-
shadowed seas.
Their music beckons, but I cannot find
The dark cathedral of the forest trees,
Nor from the night's deep chalice for my
Healing
Drink wine of strange communion, blindly
Kneeling
To pray from your omnipotence one hour
That will not perish, one immortal flower.
O Time, deal gently with me.

Winifred Holtby 1925

SECRET DIPLOMACY AMONG OLYMPIANS

Oh Aphrodite, queen of love and beauty
Hearken, I pray thee, to my humble prayer.
Allured by love and driven far by dusty duty,
I sought the Afric sun, to linger there—
Caught in the tangles of Apollo's hair,
A golden snare.

Grim Vulcan forged his swords and bitter arrows,
Fountains of light tossed in the southern air;
His molten streams through cataracts and narrows
Lift the remote recesses of his lair,
And sparkled, splintering as fine as hair,
To quiver there.

But Mercury snapped short the slender lances
And tossed to his lieutenant of the air
The army that attacks and feints and dances—
Mosquitoes fashioned for a world's despair,
The weapons forged from molten sunlight, rare
And debonair.

Thus I, who walk imperilled and assaulted,
Pray unto thee, who all my fears may share,
For the safety from the gods who thus defaulted
Pursue me by such arms I may not dare.
Send me thy doves to dissipate my care!
(Eau de Cologne, Lavender Water, Ammonia, Buzzoff and
Salts of Geranium are no use, I've tried 'em!)
Oh hear my prayer!

Winifred Holtby 1926

SEE I HAVE CAST MY NETS

See I have cast my nets
Over the ball of the world
Wherever my friends sail out on the wide seas,
Wherever their sails are furled
In hill-girt harbour, or swinging river-mouth
 My nets are hurled.

The ship brings news for me,
And the wind their words,
For my friends have enslaved the trees as their messengers,
The slow-moving herds
Of cattle, the wind-blown seeds, and the running streams,
And the homing birds.

Now all the world is mine,
China and Labrador,
Hungary, Africa, Washington, Rome
And a hundred more
Tall cities, and many a sudden-flowering isle
And a rocky shore.

For I have part in the land
Wherever my friends go.
Wherever the hills of their pilgrimage break and their cities
Tower
And their red roads glow,
I have cast my nets and drawn them home to my mind,
Though they never know.

Now have I wealth indeed,
Who hold the world in fee.
There is not a flowering field on the merry earth,
Not an almond tree,
But its beauty had gladdened the heart of a friend of mine,
And enriches me.

Winifred Holtby 1926

PARTING IS NOT SORROWFUL

Parting is not sorrowful
For such as you and me;
It only means another place
Where I should like to be,

Golden glow the roads for me,
Lands have richer worth;
Men befriend my friends for me
Over half the earth.

Foreign towns are friendly now,
Foreign fields are fair.
Half the earth is home to me,
If friends like you are there.

Winifred Holtby 1926

CELIA TO ROSALIND

Rosalind, when you and I
Walked beneath an April sky,
Trod the hidden paths between
Arden's faery forests green,
Found the groves that no man knew
Where the frail wind-flowers grew
Did we know that then we made
For ourselves a special glade
Into which our thoughts would stray
Many a hot and dusty day?
When the city lies asleep
Often still the tryst I keep,
Toss the dew-wet boughs aside
Tread the long green forest ride,
Breathe the damp and scented air—
Autumn's dower to Spring time there,
Rosalind, sometimes do you
Leave the twisted dry Karoo,
Leave the aloe spears aflame,
Leave the kopje's tortured shame,
Did you see the trees
In their green and gracious ease
Shake the shadows from their hair?
Are the daffodils still fair?
Do the squirrels scamper yet
Where the moss-grown boughs are wet;
Rosalind, when next you go,
Call to me, and I shall know—
Call, and I will run apace
To our secret trysting place—
Rosalind, where you and I
Walked beneath an April sky.

Winifred Holtby 1926

WARNING

Professor F. de Zulueta,
Descendent of that gladiator
Who slew in Spain a Procurator
For arguing from unsound data,
Is now a lofty speculator
Whose fecund sense of its creator
From Newfoundland to the Equator.

A mere forensic agitator
Must use a mental escalator
To climb to realms where Zulueta
Becomes a ruthless confiscator
Of every lesser cogitator
Who rashly dares to try has fate, or
Pursues conclusions inchoate, or
Aspiring as an innovator,
Proves a successful imitator,
Of Doctor F. de Zulueta

Winifred Holtby 1925

AVE, CEASAR!

Hail, Ceasar! We who are about to die
Salute thee, and the law which though doest give,
But were we now instead about to live,
Hail Christ, the Lord of Life, should be our cry.

In Caesar's country, laws envenom sin,
From man to man is ignorance and strife
But in the country of the Lord of Life
The only law comes from the mind within.

Those who are bound so soon for death may keep
 From day to day the covenant of fools
Fetter their passions with ignoble rules
 And stumble blindly to eternal sleep.

But we who seek the Kingdom of the Mind
Know that our wills its liberties may give;
Hail, Christ! For we who are about to live
Go now from hence, to seek until we find.

Winifred Holtby 1926

THE GRUDGING GHOST

Had I loved you more, you might
Meetly rob my days of light,
Had we loved through steadfast years
Gently then had flowed my tears.

But, unanswering heart to heart,
Lived we all our days apart.
Love was nothing in our mind
Save desire to be kind.

You are dead, and still I stand
 In the gold autumnal land.
Still I see the barley sheaves
And dance of the fallen leaves.

You are Dead, and still I meet
 Kindly faces in the street,
 Laughter, music, talk and wine
 Still are sweet and still are mine.

Grudging ghost, why must you steal
Joy from all these joys I feel?
Must you take from day to day
Gaiety and youth away?

Must you still while seasons run
Cast your shadow on the sun?
I have nothing more to give.
Sleep, ah, sleep and let me live.

Winifred Holtby 1928

AM TO THE END OF LOVE

u said that death was not the end; most true
ath was not stronger than my love for you.
t since sweet love so lightly goes, my friend,
e are not dead, and yet – this is the end.

inifred Holtby 1931

TRAINS IN FRANCE

All through the night among the unseen hills
The trains,
The fire-eyed trains
Call to each other their seeking cry,
And I,
Who thought I had forgotten all the War,
Remember now a night in Camiers,
When, through the darkness, as I wakeful lay,
I heard the trains,
The savage, shrieking trains,
Call to each other their fierce hunting-cry,
Ruthless, inevitable, as the beasts
After their prey.
Made for this end by their creators, they
Whose business was to capture and devour
Flesh of our flesh, bone of our very bone.
Hour after hour,
Angry and impotent I lay alone
Hearing them hunt you down, my dear, and you,
Hearing them carry you away to die,
Trying to warn you of the beasts, the beasts!
Then no thought I,
So foul a dream as this cannot be true
And calmed myself, hearing their cry no more.
Till, from the silence, broke a trembling roar,
And I heard, far away,
The growling thunder of their joyless feasts—
The beasts had got you then, the beasts- the beasts
And Knew
The nightmare true.

Winifred Holtby 1931

CRISIS

Is there much difference
Between the new Casino at Monte Carlo
And new International Bank at Basle ?
Do bankers know much more
About the rise and fall of Credit
Than croupiers know
About the next resting-place of their spinning ball?
Is not Roulette
And almost as expensive?
As important to those who play it
As Politics
And almost as expensive?
And what the Hell is reality, anyway,
Especially in a wet August?

Winifred Holtby 1931

THE SYMPHONY CONCERT

For me to-night they build these frozen towers,
These battlements of music, these supreme
Pinnacles carven, garlanded with flowers,
Enchanted architecture of a dream.
Yet, entering, I know that all I see
Of loveliness was never planned for me.

My footsteps stumble at the open door,
I grope along the halls with outstretched hand,
Seeing a little, and forgetting more,
Admiring where I cannot understand,
A gaping stranger, idly loitering
Round the deserted throne-room of a king.

These were your palaces;
The terraced garden to its farthest ends,
The empty corridors I wander through
Were crowded with your memories, your friends,
And not a fountain, not a cup, was wrought,
But drew fresh beauty from your mastering thought.

I am your deputy. Ah, pardon then
This dull perception, these untutored ears.
How should I hear as well as other men
Who, under every song, for thirteen years,
Have heard re-echo that last sound you knew—
The shrapnel splintering before it slew?

Winifred Holtby 1931

HOUSE ON FIRE

This house was built for grief.
Sorrow alone,
Sorrow without relief
Could make it strong,
Stiffen the crumbling clay with frequent tears,
Set firm the stone.
Impregnable throughout the weary years,
It would last long

But since with perilous joy
I reckless dwell,
Happiness will destroy
Both roof and wall,
Set the tall thatch and oaken door alight,
Till, blazing well,
Conspicuous as a torch in the dark night,
My house will fall.

Winifred Holtby 1932

ART AND SCIENCE

("Science has absolutely nothing to give Art"— An American Critic)

Must we complain of beauty who have seen
The wakening woods unfold their gowns of green,
Or the day's loveliness serenely die
Below the pale pavilion of the sky?

These having seen, are we so blindly bold
To say that beauty's little tale is told?
Rather we walk with eyes that cannot see
Her revelation in the days to be.

We shall make pictures, when we have the skill,
Of the clear crystal that the rocks distil,
And draw fair pictures to enrich our night
With inexorable curves of light.

We shall weave traceries as fine as lace
Of the minute events of time in space,
And hear through silence, with enchanted ears,
The silver music of the turning spheres.

Then shall we glory, with enfranchised sight,
In smallest wonder or superb delight,
And marvel with compassionate amaze
At these lost, blind, inert, unhearing days.

Winifred Holtby 1930

THE AEROPLANE

(Lines in the Memory of Dorothy McCalman)

This is the thought of man
Molten into steel, woven into silk.
This is the thought and the will and the courage of man
Which swings to me
Above the small beloved and chequered isle,
The green isle.
The island you peopled with cavalcades
Of knights riding to war
And kings that died.
The isle that is rich with the people of your thought.
This is your steely sea, dappled with cloud,
Flecked with white cuckoo-spit,
These are your little tossing boats like water beatles
Scurrying hither and thither.
I too have left the earth,
I too will follow.

My silver wings careen towards the field,
My swooping wings scoop up the stubbled hill;
The form of the field lies plastic to my will,
I mould the hills and hollow the valleys, I—
I have left the earth. I have sought the heavenly sky.
This is better than life, and if this, this is to die,
Then I will follow you I—
I too, will die.

Winifred Holtby 1930

NB: Dorothy McCalman was a friend of Winifred Holtby who Winifred
helped after she was dispossessed by her family after converting to
Catholicism. Dorothy achieved her degree from Oxford but sadly died
shortly afterwards.

THE GHOST OF ELINOR WYLIE
1. ESCORT

Not when you glittered, royally attended,
Gallant and debonaire,
By brilliant words and dancing mirth be-
Friended;
I was not with you there.

But roused by pain, in the abysmal hour
When angry pulses leap,
And black blood lashes its frustrated power
Against tall cliffs of sleep;

Then, when the hounds of fear sprang from the
Shadows
In horror's hue and cry
Hot on your heels, through the grey morning
Meadows
Hunting you down to die;

Then, when you thought that there was none
Beside you,
No prince or poet near,
Only the silver sunrise to deride you
And your pulsating fear;

Then, when you turned, by livid moonlight
Sickened,
Seeking the hidden sign—
My breath it was upon your breath that quickened;
the fear, the pain, were mine.

Winifred Holtby 1932

NB: Winifred Holtby wrote these three poems when she was recovering from the first attack of the illness that eventually proved fatal. An illness very similar which affected Elinor Wylie an American Poetess from which she eventually died.

THE GHOST OF ELINOR WYLIE
II. CORONATION

Must you have roses for your coronation?
Orchids like butterflies,
Exotic lilies, and the clove carnation
That bleeds before it dies?

I have made you a wreath that is not of the laurel
 No laurels or bays are mine.
My flowers are bindweed and the rusty sorrel,
Mallow and eglantine

I have twisted my travellers joy above your portal
For traveller's joy is rest;
I have plucked for you thyme, since, now you
Are immortal,
Quick-fading time's a jest.

And out of these I have woven a wreath and
Crowned you
Below your delicate feet
I have spread my feathery grasses, and all
Around you
My wild wold flowers smell sweet.

My herbs are plain; but their stems are all the stronger.
And look! I offer you
Poppies, to make your quiet sleep last longer,
Mandragora and rue.

Winifred Holtby 1932

THE GHOST OF ELINOR WYLIE
III. PEACE

Put up your bright sword; you have done with fighting.
Your enemies are fled.
There's no more need for mirth, nor joy's
Requiting
Among the quiet dead.

The wounds are healed now and the wrongs
Are mended;
Now, the brave battle of your laughter ended,
You, if you will, may weep.

Your terraced garden, your fantastic palaces
Were all too high, too cold;
Bitter the wine you drank from crystal chalices,
Heavy the carven gold.

Your glass and silver were too faery brittle,
Your silk brocades too thin
Come, you may warm yourself down here a little,
With a shroud to ease your pain,
And in the grave you'll find sufficient reason
To turn and sleep again.

Winifred Holtby 1932

RESURRECTION

He had been free,
He had looked into the clear face of death and known salvation.
As a bather strips before diving he had stripped
Himself of desire, memory and sorrow,
He had stood poised above the lucid water,
The sea of oblivion spread itself before him,
The kingdoms of the world fell back behind him
like a grey swallow, like a small wraith of smoke
Their hopes, their powers, their pleasures, their excitement.

Winifred Holtby
Hull

KINDLINESS

Had I loved you more you might
Meetly rob my days of light
Had we loved through thirty years
Tranquil then had been my tears.

But unanswering heart to heart,
Lived we all our days apart
Love was nothing your mind
Save the desire to be kind.

Mournful friendship would not give
Kindliness so that love might live.
But in sharp contention shows
Loves more lovely than the rose.

Friendship is no friend to suthe,
Friendship words with burning truth
Friendship stings with sharpened pain.
Till dwell kindliness is slain.

Loves eternal, urgent strife
Cannot end mortal life.
Kindliness is kin to death
End in with the end of breath.

Kindliness between us lies
Life with shadow on our eyes
Let the worst of it be said:
You were kind, and you are dead;

I am living and I find
Life to death is never kind
Had you loved me more you might
Metely rob my days of light.

Winifred Holtby
Hull

MALEDICTION AGAINST HUMILITY

Ask of the rose, only that it should glow
With natural beauties such as roses know
Ask of the stars only that they should shine
With a glittering patterns such as stars design,
Ask of the moon only that it should rise
With tranquillity of paradise.
ut to ask less, is not to ask enough.

You ask too little when you ask my mind
Only to be perpetually kind,
You ask too little when you ask my heart
Only to dwell in faithfulness apart,
Kindness and faith mean little into those
Who know the royal splendours of the rose;
And to ask less, is not to ask enough.

If stars and roses and the transient moon
Fling with wide their largesse to the night and moon;
If hearts are proud as princes and must give
Royally that their regal love may live;
Shame on your mean conception of the will,
To ask so little, and to ask it ill!
For to ask for less, is not to ask enough.

Winifred Holtby
Hull

BEAUTY THE WAY OF THE WORLD

Never mind now. You have done all that was needful,
You have given my eyes their blue and my hair its gold;
You have taught my body to move with a grace unheedful,
I am beautiful now, I shall not grow old.

You have made me sure of myself and I am grateful.
"I too was adored once" now once is enough
Why should you look at me, then as at one grown fateful?
Why should your voice grow harsh and your gesture rough.

Have I not thanked you well for your gift of beauty?
See I acknowledge it. I am your work of art
You modelled this gold, this rose and this pearl to suit 'ee
Is it my fault, if you say that I have no heart.

Did you teach my tongue to be kind and my fingers tender?
Did you ask me to spill my sweetness to quench your flame?
You cried to my lips, "Be red"! to my hands be slender
They have obeyed, you have only yourself to blame.

Winifred Holtby
Hull

VALLEY OF THE SHADOWS

The hours creep slowly by, the afternoon
Comes slower still, the sleepy minutes pass
In order by, to be forgotten soon:
What will ye have the morning bring you?
The hours are slow, but till they pass away.
They never will return, how'er we long
To live again some idle, mis-spent day.
They never will return, but only this
I ask, that we can spend a few more hours
Together, that we may have one more kiss.
Once more, then, sleep. Ah! Child, but life is good:
It seemeth hard when I have thee, to die!
I almost wish the days, instead of ling' ring
Towards the appointed hour of death would fly
And it is sweet to lie among the grasses
With you beside me – after years of pain:
With thrushes singing round us; yes 'tis pleasant;
It makes me almost wish to live again.
Well, didst thou come before the ordered hour;
Well, not well, for thou has given me fear,
If I must die I e'en must do it willing,
But thou hast made me wish to live on, dear.
How long we loved! How sweet amid the flowers
Wast thou when I first saw these! ah! How sweet!
The hawthorn blossoms on high above these;
The daisies grew beneath thy dainty feet;
Where thou hast trod, dear heart, little petals
Turned crimson to their tips with love of you;
The sweet forget-me-nots owned you as gracious,
And spread thy paths with coverlits of blue.
Nay, weep not, sweet 'twas you that taught me faith;
And by your life of love and steadfastness,
You taught me God is sweeter far than fame;
You taught me, not by words, but by your own
Sweet gentleness, that love bridged many things,

And yet it was not all, but honour more;
More than our love, more than all it brings;
So dear, I left you and my happiness,
And wandered far, thought much, and loved you still,
And knew that you would not forsake me now,
When I returned dear heart old sad and ill.
Nay, weep not, dear, 'twas you that made me go
And just for you that I came back to die.
You taught me that my life was thrown away –
That there were other lives more true and high.
Bend over me. How beautiful thou art!
How sweet, how pure, my wife, my bride, my dear
You say that, after death, we meet again;
Were it not so, death without you were drear.
Nay child, you own sweet words, 'We meet again;
'Death cannot part us, we are both one!'
Death shall not part us, love has bridged all things;
Let it go on, e'en as it has begun.
My life is little, dear – not great or grand.
Sigh for me, for in a little while
'We meet again'; you said so dry those tears
And e'er I die, give me but one more smile.
Ah! How I love thee! Yes we meet again,
But not yet darling dearest not just yet.
In prayer unto that mighty God of thine,
In Him, my darling, learn how to forget;
And if it comforts thee, when I am gone,
Remember how thy noble heart and life
Kept one poor wretch from misery and shame,
And from the curse of a dishonoured strife.
Think how thy life is still of use to men;
Think how I loved you; know I love you still.
Give me your promise you will not despair;
Give it, my love, here where the thrushes trill.
See how the sun shines out between the clouds,
So shines my love in this world's blacker night --
If love were all – but honour, it is more
Look up, my love – look up – 'tis light' tis light.

Winifred Holtby, Hull

HAPPY ENDING

Ah, close the chapter on this hour,
So green the grass, the air so sweet,
All spring time burning in a flower,
All summer blossoming at our feel.

Though what's to come be past our mending,
All that has been has led to this;
Then give the tale the happy ending,
And close the chapter with a kiss.

What if estrangements follow the greetings?
What if our lovely loves grow cold?
Since journeys end in lovers meetings,
Keep silence now; this tale is told.

Winifred Holtby 1932

EPILOGUE

After the death of Winifred Holtby, a letter remains in her papers at Hull University, written by Harry Pearson to her mother Alice Holtby. In it he says that he had been reading the letters Winifred had sent to him and he came to the conclusion that" Winifred's success was not just mere success", which it wasn't. Winifred Holtby through out her life never allowed whatever success she achieved to cloud her judgement and sway her from the issues that she fought for, feminism, equality of race, pacifism and those less fortunate than herself. Although Harry Pearson caused Winifred a great deal of mental anguish and unhappiness throughout her life, she always forgave his wayward ways. Thus it is that he was the only man that she really loved.

Harry Pearson in his letter to Alice Holtby dedicated this poem to Winifred:

> Somewhere among those lovely sleeping hills
> You dwell;
> And if I wander to the highest rills,
> And call you by the name we loved so well,
> From hill to hill your voice would ring as clear
> As though you were here.
>
>
> But not till daylight trembles into dusk,
> And earth and sky are knit in harmony,
> And the stillness like soft rain descends,
> And time is lost in beauty's heart;
> Not till then,
> I see you as a part
> Of sunset and the vast silence of the stars.